GEORGE RITACCO

This book is designed to provide information that the author believes to be accurate on the subject matter it covers, but it is sold with the understanding that neither the author nor the publisher is offering individualized advice tailored to any specific business or to any individual's particular needs, or rendering advice or other professional services. A competent professional's services should be sought if one needs expert assistance.

Every effort has been made to make all publications and products sold through this site or through phone and mail as complete and accurate as possible. However, there may be mistakes both typographical and in content. Therefore, this text should be used only as a general guide and not as the ultimate reference source.

This publication references data and experiences collected over many time periods. Past results do not guarantee future performance. This book solely provides historical data to discuss and illustrate the underlying principles. Additionally, this book is not intended to serve as the basis for any financial decision.

No warranty is made with respect to the accuracy or completeness of the information contained herein, and both the author and the publisher specifically disclaim any responsibility for any liability, loss, or risk, personal or otherwise, which is incurred as a consequence, directly or indirectly, of the use and application of any of the contents of this book.

For more information please email
George.ritacco@globalvisiontech.com

PRINTING HISTORY
George Ritacco - Global Market Distribution / 2015

Manufactured in the United States of America

# DISCLAIMER

We wrote this book with a very practical mindset. We wanted to do more than just tell you about the "why" of case management — as it relates to strategy, database management and workflow for your caseworkers. We also wanted to share with you the "how" — the tactics. We wanted to take our collective experience with thousands of users, including our own and turn it into something that you can use and leverage for better results and better outcomes.

However, before we shared any of practical uses of software and databases, we needed to start with a foundation, a current state of the long term care industry and where the LTC, home health care and elderly care industries are heading in order for our message to make the most sense in today's environment.

We hope you enjoy the book and are able to use it to dramatically transform your organization's approach to information management.

-George Ritacco
George.ritacco@globalvisiontech.com
twitter.com/gvtinc
famcare.net/blog

WELCOME TO THE AGING TIDAL WAVE

# ACKNOWLEDGEMENTS

Thank you to the following people who helped birth this book and who, without their contributions and support, this book would not have been written:

For their inspiration - Jimmy Harding, as a coach and mentor and his advice that writing a book was a good thing; my grandmother Elizabeth Ritacco and my wife's grandmother Virginia Calnan, who both lived well into their 90s and spent their final days in a long term care facility. They both inspired me to take a deeper look into our solutions and see if there was a better way.

To my family — my wife, Danielle, and my two wonderful children, Jack and Olivia, for their continued love and support.

For the mountains of research material he poured through and his copywriting expertise — Francis Bennett.

For their tutelage, guidance, patience and innovative software platform — April & Chris Freund and the Global Vision Technologies development team.

# Welcome to The Aging TIDAL WAVE

**This is an Interactive Book with Free Videos, Case Studies and Other Useful Tools!**

Please register by visiting the website, register, introduce yourself, share what you do and your biggest problem that you'd like to tackle with information management.

On this site you can see free videos and an opportunity to get a free, one-hour consultation (a $150 value) with a seasoned, FAMCare specialist.

Visit: http://try.famcare.net/megaresources
or send an email to: info@globalvisiontech.com
or call: 678-965-6821

# CONTENTS

# ABOUT THE AUTHOR

George Ritacco is the Executive Director of Client Services at Global Vision Technologies, Inc. (GVT). GVT helps others leverage technology to benefit themselves and improve the outcomes for the clients they serve. They do this with a suite of business and software tools designed to answer the challenges and opportunities of caseworkers and agency and program directors in the human services industry.

If you are interested in learning more about our solutions, our latest projects and/or thoughts on the industry, there is plenty more to read, watch and ponder at www.globalvisiontech.com and www.famcare.net.

## ABOUT THIS BOOK

The Baby Boom Generation looms over the long-term care industry like a tidal wave. Every year, for the next twenty years, 3 million of the 75 million baby boomers born between 1946 and 1964 will hit retirement age (Barr, 2014). By 2029, when the last round of "boomers" retires, the number of Americans 65 or older will climb to more than **71 million** (Colby & Ortman, 2014). In other words, we are looking at a tidal wave of more than 30 million additional retirees in the next fifteen years.

Currently, long-term care service providers serve approximately 8 million people (Harris-Kojetin, Sengupta, Park-Lee, &Valverde, 2013). However, by 2050, the number of people using nursing facilities, alternative residential care places, or home care services, however, is projected to exceed 27 million (Evashwick, Frates & Fahey, 2008).

The long-term care industry is simply not preparing to serve this sudden spike in the elderly population. So far, the growth in the number of senior citizen boomers has been incremental, and its impact on health care has been overshadowed by federal reform and budget battles. "This is the most powerful force operating in our health system right now, this generational change," says Jeff Goldsmith, president of Health Futures Inc., Charlottesville, Va. "But, people aren't paying much attention" (Barr, 2014).

The purpose of this book is to alert the long-term care industry to the baby boom tidal wave cresting on our shores. By comparing the current capacity and projected growth of long-term care facilities, staffing, and finance with the future care requirements of retiring baby boomers, we hope to demonstrate the dramatic shortages that threaten a complete collapse of service.

Like the answer to global warming or the continued exclusive use of fossil fuels to supply the world's energy needs, only creative innovation will enable the long-term care industry to survive this population tidal wave. Simply expanding the current system with its limitations and inadequacies will not work (Applebaum & Kunkel, 1991).

At the time of the writing of this book — the verdict is still out on the Affordable Care Act and what impact it will have on our society.

We've attempted to outline the current "state of affairs" — not only the potential outcomes if the situation is left un-checked, but also the solutions that will either eradicate and/or fix critical issues and help you better plan for what's to come.

# INTRODUCTION

## BACK TO THE FUTURE

*An Interview with Ben Goodman*

Ben "Benny" Goodman is a dashing 72 year-old retired auto dealer from Phoenix, Arizona. With his carefully trimmed Fu Manchu and wavy white hair he's a dead ringer for Sean Connery in his later years. A "let's do this" kind of guy, he took over his father's original dealership in Mesa, Arizona and built the business into a regional powerhouse.

"I was surprised when Peggy died," he said during our first interview. "I shouldn't have been. She had been ill. But, you know, when you live with the person you love for almost fifty years they become permanent in your head. But suddenly, Peg was gone and for the first time in my life I didn't know what to do. I was ridiculous. I didn't even know what to eat for breakfast. I'd come down here to the kitchen and wander around looking through the fridge and the cabinets for ideas," he said with a smile. "I would roam around the house like a stranger wondering what to do with all these rooms. I had never even been in some of the bedrooms. I would think, "I wonder what Peg was doing with all this stuff."

"How did the idea of a group home occur to you?" I asked.

"Completely by accident," he replied. "I still go down to the dealership every day and shoot the breeze with some of the older guys working there. I've always loved cars and everything to do with them. I like to see what's selling and which models bombed; discuss the new technology with the old guys. They're surprisingly excited about each new computer gizmo the engineers stick in.

"Well, anyway, one day, Ernie Sprool, the maintenance manager, brings up Evelyn Fishbinder. Evelyn was the first woman mechanic to work in a dealership, maybe anywhere in the country, but certainly here in Phoenix. My father hired her back in the 60's, and she rose to be maintenance shop foreman and ran the shop in Mesa for almost thirty years. She's 91 now, and for the last twenty-five years had been living in a tiny shack out in Apache Junction. Anyway, Ernie told me that poor old Evelyn was losing her eyesight and was having trouble taking care of herself like she always had.

"Well, almost instantly, I decided to go out to Apache Junction and see how I could help her. After all, ever since I was boy, she had been a living legend in my life. But what I found changed my life. The old lady was as thin as a rail, hadn't washed in days, and couldn't even clean her little shack. She was literally sitting there waiting to die. This was the same woman who was considered the best mechanic in Phoenix and ran a twenty-man maintenance department brooking no nonsense while she was at it. I immediately took her home with me."

"That's how this all started?" I asked.

"Pretty much," he said, smiling. "I just hired a home health aide to look after Evelyn and off we went. Maggie is her name and she is great! Evelyn, of course, protested and insisted on paying her way with her social security and a little pension. It was just a gesture on her part, but it got me to thinking about the other three empty bedrooms and the fact that I already had a home health aide on the payroll. Like I said, Maggie is great and she takes great care of our family. She visits with them often and keeps her notes in one of those IPad things. She says she uses a database that helps her manage the information and the care she provides to each of us. Technology, huh?  Watching her type reminds me of an old Star Trek episode and seeing Lt. Uhura type information into her tricorder. Gosh…we sure have come a long way! Anyway — getting back to how all of this started . . . I thought, you know, I could put this big house to good use, and each person could pay a part of the cost. I thought that would be a good thing to do, and I was going stir crazy anyway, so why not? After a few months with Evelyn already in residence, I went looking for another old person who might need a little support."

"Where did you look?" I asked.

"Well, right under my nose, you might say. My entire life, I went to the same barber. — Tony Mancuso. Tony's Barber Shop was not one of these fancy New Age deals with hair dryers and facial messages and ninety-dollar haircuts for balding men. No sir. Tony's was a five dollar haircut in the old days and never got over twenty dollars till the day he retired. I guess by today's standards you didn't get much haircut, but you got plenty of gossip, sports, and jokes. Tony was a great old guy. Worked till he was seventy but then the arthritis got him. A year later, his wife dies and there's no one to look after him. He ends up for a couple of months in an assisted living facility but the money runs out, and I find him living all alone in a dingy motel with drug addicts and hookers. So he's here now and driving old Evelyn nuts with jokes she never gets. His social security is enough to feed him and helps pay for the home health aide."

"Is she the lady I saw out back tending the garden?"

"Oh, no; she's another story," Ben said with a sigh. "That's Sister Mary Patrick; taught my kids over at Xavier. Did you know that some nuns have no retirement? I never knew that. Her order disbanded back in the 90's, and she ended up with no place to live. All her family is gone, and she couldn't find a job at her age. She insists on doing all the gardening to supplement her meager social security payment, and I got the Church to kick in a little since she had nothing. I let her do the gardening because it makes her feel good about herself. She's still pretty independent in her own head. Can you imagine a fine, educated woman like that left with nothing at the end of her life?"

At this point in the interview, Ben took me on a tour of his lovely Santa Fe style home. It has five bedrooms and four bathrooms with an enormous formal dining room, living room, and an expansive family room separated from the outdoor patio and pool by a wall of glass doors. "I realized that I had the perfect place to turn into a small group home. Everybody isn't as fortunate to have such a big place, but even more modest homes could easily be put to the same use. It's the perfect answer, really, to what is becoming a big problem," he said as we entered the family room to meet the fourth resident.

"I would like you to meet Lieutenant Willie Brogan of the 82nd Airborne Division, retired," Ben said as we walked around in front of an old man in a wheelchair. Lieutenant Brogan was a husky, bald guy.

"How do you do?" he said in a courtly manner that didn't quite go with his rugged physical appearance. "We don't get many visitors these days; nice to see a new face."

"A pleasure," I said shaking his hand.

"Ben tells me you're writing a book about us," he said.

"Well, I'm preparing a report, a small book on Long-Term Care," I said. "It's not really a book about anyone in particular."

"Well, never mind. You've come to the right place. We're certainly trying to care for one another for the long haul; not much haul left in any of us, if you ask me, but while we're all still here we try to look after one another."

As we walked back to the kitchen, Ben told me that Lieutenant Brogan served with his brother in Vietnam. He had been knocking around all these years with no permanent place to live until Ben's brother called and asked if he had room for one more. "I sure did, and Willie's been here ever since."

"I'm not running a charity here," Ben said later. "Sure, I realize that I might be a little more fortunate than most, so I can contribute this home to the cause. But everyone here contributes their retirement and social security and any other benefit they might have and that all goes to pay the home health aide and buy food. It's working out real good for everybody, including me.

"I made a lot of money selling cars, but, you know, I never did it for the money. Oh, I was glad for it, don't get me wrong. But I really loved cars and putting people behind the wheel of a car I knew they would love. That's what kept me excited about everything.

"I'm getting the same excitement sharing Peg's home with wonderful people who I have known and loved my whole life. That's the real payoff for me. I'm not rattling around alone wondering what to do with all this stuff and myself. I know what to do. You see? There's the payoff."

Before I left, I explained to Ben that Long-Term Care as an industry only started with the Social Security Act of 1935 and the addition of Medicare in 1965. Before that, families and local communities had to find ways to care for the elderly and disabled just like he was currently doing in Phoenix.

We believe the future of long-term care could one day be in the hands of people that share Ben Goodman's heart and mind. It is one solution to a tremendous problem that is at our doorstep. Along with creative and innovative ways to position new "facilities" — such as a group home approach as described by Ben — there are financial and technological solutions.

In the next few chapters you will encounter specific data that indicates the long-term care industry is about to be inundated, flooded and swamped. The data is scary and if left unchecked, it can spell doom or c-o-l-l-a-p-s-e for the entire eldercare industry.

The Baby Boom Generation is about to overwhelm the institutional government-supported structure of the Long-Term Care industry. As you will see from the data, a return to caring for the aged on a local level with some government financial support may well become the "new normal."

*"Just remember, once you're over the
hill – you begin to pick up speed!"*

*~Arthur Schopenhauer*

# CHAPTER ONE

## The Current Face of Long Term Care

### *DEFINITION OF LONG TERM CARE*

The long-term care industry and long-term care services include a broad range of health care, personal care, and supportive services that meet the needs of frail older people and other adults whose capacity to carry out basic self-care tasks, called activities of daily living (ADLs)(e.g. bathing, dressing or eating), or instrumental activities of daily living (IADLs)(e.g. household chores, meal preparation, or managing money) is limited because of a chronic illness; injury; physical, cognitive, or mental disability; or other health-related conditions (Harris-Kojetin et al, 2013).

### *EXISTING FACILITIES*

A long-term care facility provides rehabilitative, restorative, and/or ongoing skilled nursing care to patients or residents in need of assistance with activities of daily living.

In 2012, 58,500 long-term care service providers served approximately **8 million** people in the United States (Harris-Kojetin et al, 2013).

**1. Group Homes** are small, private facilities where residents can live in private or shared rooms. Residents receive personal care, meals, and have staff available around the clock. Nursing and medical care is not usually provided on site (LTC: Facility Based Services, 2011).

**2. Nursing Homes:** Currently, 15,700 nursing homes provide a wide range of health and personal care services to over one million residents who receive increased medical care, nursing care, 24-hour supervision, three meals a day, and assistance with everyday activities (Harris-Kojetin et al, 2013). Rehabilitation services such as physical, occupational, and speech therapy are also available. Although nursing homes are still a major provider of long-term care services, there is growing use of skilled nursing facilities for short-term, post-acute care and rehabilitation (LTC: FBS, 2011).

**3. Assisted Living Facilities**: There are approximately 31,100 facilities serving over one million people who need help with daily care, but do not need as much help as a nursing home provides. (Harris-Kojetin et al, 2013). Typically, a few "levels of care" are offered, with residents paying more for higher levels of care. Residents have access to many services, including up to three meals a day; assistance with personal care; help with medications, housekeeping and laundry; 24-hour supervision, security, and onsite staff; and social and recreational activities (LTC: FBS, 2011).

**4. Continuing Care Retirement Communities, (CCRCs),** are also called life care communities, and offer residents a full range of housing choices and services on one campus (LTC: Facility Based Services, 2011). A resident can move between levels of care as needed, progressing from independent living to assisted living and on to skilled nursing if necessary. (LTC: Facility Based Services, 2011) There are currently more than 700,000 residents living in over 22,200 facilities nationwide (Harris-Kojetin et al, 2013).

**FIGURE #1:** **Residential Care Statistics 2012**

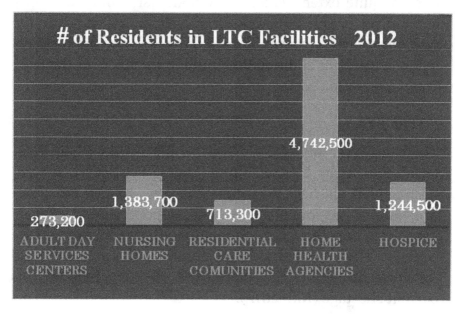

**DATA SOURCE**: Harris-Kojetin, Ph.D., L., Sengupta, Ph.D., M., Park-Lee, Ph.D., E., & Valverde, M.P.H., R. (2013, January 1). Long-Term Care Services in the United States: 2013 Overview.

**5. Hospice** agencies operate 3,700 inpatient facilities nationwide (Harris-Kojetin et al, 2013). Most of these facilities are either freestanding or located on a hospital campus and give support to people in the final stages of a terminal illness. Short-term inpatient care can be made available when pain or symptoms become too difficult to manage at home, or the caregiver needs respite. In 2012, hospice facilities served over one million patients (Harris-Kojetin et al, 2013).

**6. Home Health Agencies**: 17,000 Home Health Agencies and Adult Day Service Centers provide the bulk of services to over five million seniors who remain in their own homes (Harris-Kojetin et al, 2013).

The existing ad hoc network of long-term care facilities is already quite extensive and serves almost 8 million elderly and infirm patients (Harris-Kojetin et al, 2013). Over the next 20 years, however, it will be rendered dramatically inadequate as an additional 27 million members of the baby boom generation seek care.

## *STAFFING*

There are currently 5.2 million people employed in long-term care in the United States. There is, however, a well-documented shortage of competent professional and para-professional personnel to manage, supervise, and provide long-term care services in facility-based and home care settings. High turnover, large numbers of vacancies, and difficulty attracting new employees all contribute to this current shortage (Rill, 2012).

The shortage is responsible for service access problems that threaten patient's safety, quality of care, and quality of life. It is also adding to excessive costs as providers continuously recruit and train new personnel and use temporary, higher cost contract staff. Extreme workloads for both nurses and paraprofessional staff, inadequate supervision, less time for new staff to learn their jobs, and high accident and injury rates are dramatically affecting the quality of care (Rill, 2012).

# Physicians

There are currently 4,278 physicians in the United States specializing in Geriatric Medicine. These physicians carry the third highest number of patients (72, 242) per physician (2012 Physician Specialty DBWS). In 2009, 44% of geriatric medicine fellowship training programs were unfilled. For clinical training, family physicians are only required to take 12 days of geriatric training, 20 days for internal medicine residency, and 23 days for geriatric psychiatry. As a result, only 6,600 of the 650,000 physicians are certified in geriatrics (Rill, 2012).

Geriatrics is also one of the lower-paid medical specialties, in part because virtually all its patients are on Medicare, which pays doctors less than commercial insurers (SPAN, 2013). In other words, Geriatric Medicine is the least popular of all available specialties because geriatricians are both over-worked and underpaid.

By one estimate, Geriatrics needs about 36,000 practitioners to care for the elderly properly (SPAN Foundation, 2012). With only 3,367 active in patient care at the present time, many experts fear that, with the enormous burst of baby boomers beginning to retire, the situation is, in fact, hopeless (2012 Physician's Specialty Data Book).

Currently the primary role of physicians involved in long-term care is as nursing home and home health agency medical directors who are required to sign off on nursing home and home health care plans (SPAN, 2012). Since 1990, nursing homes reimbursed by Medicare or Medicaid are required to have a physician medical director who is responsible for implementing medical care policies and coordinating medical care. However, 86 percent of these physicians spent less than 8 hours per week in a facility and

62 percent reported visiting the facility only once a week (Institute for the Future of Aging Services, 2007).

Clearly, physicians are not actively involved in long-term care. This lack of interest has already depressed the quality of geriatric care and will escalate to a crisis as millions of more elderly enter the long-term care system.

## Nurses

In 2012, nearly 1.5 million nursing employee full-time equivalents (FTEs) were working in long-term care. Of these nursing employees, approximately two-thirds worked in nursing homes, one-fifth were employees of residential care communities, one-tenth were employed by home health agencies and less than one-twentieth were employed by hospices and adult day services centers (LTC: FBS, 2011).

High turnover and vacancy rates, and difficulty recruiting and retaining RNs and LPNs are reported across the spectrum of long-term care providers. A survey of nursing homes conducted by the American Health Care Association found annual turnover among RNs averaged almost 49 percent, while LPN turnover averaged more than 50 percent (Harris-Kojetin et al, 2013). Facility respondents reported that 18.4 percent of RN positions were vacant, as were 14.4 percent of LPN positions (Institute for the Future of Aging Services, 2007).

A study of RN turnover in home health agencies as reported by the U.S. General Accounting Office found a 21 percent annual turnover rate. The final report of the National Commission on Nursing Workforce for Long-Term Care estimated that 96, 000 new nurses are needed just to fill current nursing home vacancies (IFAS, 2007).

# Figure #2: Total Number & Percent Distribution of Nursing Employee FTEs (Full-time equivalents) by Provider Type & Staff Type: United States, 2012

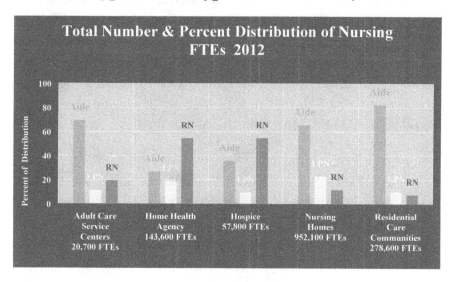

NOTES: Only employees are included for all staff types; contract staff are not included. For adult day services centers & residential care communities, aides refer to certified nursing assistants, home health aides, home care aides, personal care aides, personal care assistants, & medication technicians or medication aides. For home health agencies & hospices, aides refer to home health aides. For nursing homes, aides refer to certified nurse aides, medication aides, & medication technicians. See Technical Notes for information on how outliers were identified & coded. Percentages may not add to 100 because of rounding. Percentages are based on the unrounded numbers. FTE is full-time equivalent. SOURCES: CDC/NCHS, National Study of Long-Term Care Providers and Table 2 in Appendix B.

DATA SOURCE: Harris-Kojetin, Ph.D., L., Sengupta, Ph.D., M., Park-Lee, Ph.D., & Valverde, M.P.H., R. (2013, January 1). Long-Term Care Services in the United States: 2013 Overview.

It is clear that both physicians and nurses prefer other specialties to long-term care. The nature of the work, the pay, the hours, and the working conditions all influence this bias away from long-term care. The bulk of the care, therefore, is being provided by the paraprofessionals.

## Paraprofessionals

Paraprofessionals are considered the "hands, voice and face" of long-term care, responsible for helping frail and disabled older adults carry out the most basic activities of daily life. While the majority of paraprofessionals work in nursing homes and assisted living facilities, increasing numbers provide in-home supportive and health-related services. According to BLS data, the total paraprofessional direct care workforce in both the health and long-term care sectors consists of:

- 1,391,430 nurse aides, orderlies and attendants, largely employed in nursing homes (IFAS, 2007)
- 663,280 home health aides, a slight majority of whom work in home-based care settings (IFAS, 2007)
- 566,860 personal care and home care aides, two-thirds of whom work in home-based services (IFAS, 2007)

Vacancies and turnover are a serious problem in the paraprofessional staff as well as the nursing staff. A Wisconsin study found turnover rates among paraprofessionals of 77% in direct care, 164% in assisted living, from 99% to 127% in nursing homes, and 25% to 50% in home health agencies (IFAS, 2007). Turnover and job dissatisfaction are clearly linked to poor pay and benefits.

The paraprofessional staff are not trained, treated or paid like professionals (IFAS, 2007). Even minimal entry fast food jobs offer more upward mobility than long-term care.

# FIGURE #3: Paraprofessionals In Long Term Care - Percent Of Annual Turnover

**( ) Indicate mean average of available high & low percentages**

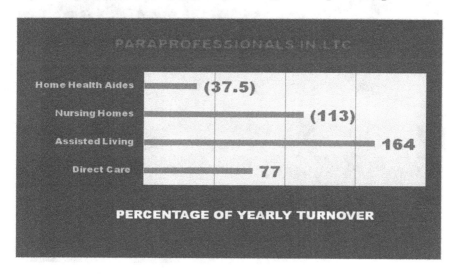

**DATA SOURCE**: Institute for the Future of Aging Services, *The Long-Term Care Workforce: Can the Crisis be Fixed?* 2007

Research confirms that the most important reason direct care paraprofessional workers stay in their jobs is the relationships they have with older adults in their care (Applebaum & Kunkel, 1991). Turnover and job dissatisfaction are clearly linked to poor pay and benefits (IFAS, 2007).

There is a serious shortage of long-term care professional and paraprofessional workers. When laid against the burgeoning needs of the next twenty years, we have entered a crisis stage.

## FIGURE #4: Wage Comparison for Jobs with Minimal Entry Requirements

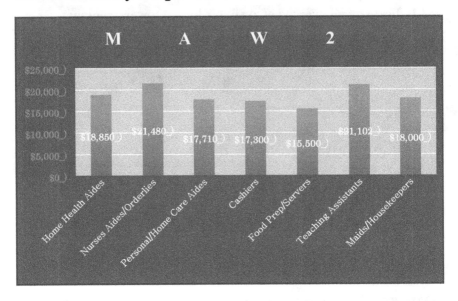

**DATA SOURCE**: Institute for the Future of Aging Services. (2007, January 1). The Long-Term Care Workforce: Can the Crisis be Fixed?

# *FINANCE*

## Current Expenditures

When Medicaid was created on July 30th, 1965, the entire GDP of the United States was $791.1 billion. No one could have predicted that by 2013 the U.S. would spend over $2 trillion on health care alone in a single year (Orestis, 2014).

Nearly $725 billion is spent per year on long-term care. Most residents pay out-of-pocket for assisted living, with a small percentage using Medicaid to help pay for services. The largest single payer for long-term nursing home care is Medicaid, whereas Medicare finances hospice costs and a major portion of the costs for short-stay, post-acute care in skilled nursing facilities. State budgets have been impacted particularly hard by shrinking tax dollars and growing Medicaid enrollment brought on by the economic crisis and an aging population (SCAN Foundation, 2013).

Despite the preference of older people for home and community-based services, the long term care financing and delivery system is biased towards institutional care (Johnson & Weiner, 2007).

Over 10 million Americans now require long-term care annually and Medicaid, the primary source of coverage, now spends $130 billion every year. Medicare, in its post-acute account spends $64 billion and Veterans, State, and local programs spend $10 billion (SCAN Foundation, 2013).

Medicaid and Medicare expenditures will increase with the growing need for long-term care services. The U.S. Congressional Budget Office projected that Medicare and Medicaid expenditures will roughly triple in constant-dollar terms between 2000 and 2040 (SCAN Foundation, 2013).

With 10,000 baby boomers turning 65 every day for the next twenty years, the United States has officially crossed the tipping point into the long feared era of the "long term care funding crisis" (SCAN, 2013).

## Long-term Care Insurance

Medicare does not cover long-term care and only about 9 percent of the population ages 55 and older have any form of private long-term care insurance (Frank, 2012).

Nevertheless, the largest provider of long-term care insurance pays $4,300,000 in benefits every business day as of April 2012. Estimates of total daily payout range from $9-$15 million when considering the entire market (Frank, 2012). The average claim is $48,000 and 71% of the claims are paid to female claimants (LTC Insurance Statistics, 2014). While 43% of claims are for one year or less, the percentage of claims lasting beyond 5 years **tripled** to approximately 15% in 2012 (LTC Insurance Statistics, 2014).

## FIGURE # 5:

# $725 BILLION SPENT ANNUALLY

**DATA SOURCE:** The State of Long-Term Care Financing, (2013), retrieved from thescanfoundation.org/infographics

# WELCOME TO THE AGING TIDAL WAVE

**This is an Interactive Book with Free Videos, Case Studies and Other Useful Tools!**

Please register by visiting the website, register, introduce yourself, share what you do and your biggest problem that you'd like to tackle with information management.

On this site you can see free videos and an opportunity to get a free, one-hour consultation (a $150 value) with a seasoned, FAMCare specialist.

Visit: http://try.famcare.net/megaresources
or send an email to: info@globalvisiontech.com
or call: 678-965-6821

*"The baby boomers are getting older, and will stay older for longer. And they will run right into the dementia firing range. How will a society cope? Especially a society that can't so readily rely on those stable family relationships that traditionally provided the backbone of care?"*

*~Terry Pratchett*

# CHAPTER TWO

## Attack of the Baby Boomers

### *TIDAL WAVE*

The number of births recorded during the years immediately following World War II was unprecedented. The National Center for Health Statistics recorded 2.9 million births in 1945, which increased by almost 20% to 3.4 million in 1946 (Barr, 2014). Births continued to increase through the rest of the 1940s and into the 1950s, reaching a peak of 4.3 million in 1957 (Colby & Ortman, 2014). By 1965 the baby boom ended and births fell below the 4 million mark (Barr, 2014).

In 1946 there were approximately 2.4 million baby boomers. By 1964, the last year of the baby boom, that figure had reached just shy of 72.5 million (Barr, 2014). Due to immigration into the United States, the size of the population born during the baby boom years continued to increase between 1965 and 1999, peaking at 78.8 million in 1999 (Colby & Ortman, 2014).

In 2011, this largest generation in history began turning 65 and 10,000 Americans will turn 65 every day from now until

2029. By 2030, when the last baby boomers turn 65, the number of Americans age 65 and older is projected to be about 72 million, roughly 19% of the total U.S. population. By 2050, the percentage of the U.S. population that is age 85 and older is expected to grow by 126%. 17.9 million Americans will be 85 or older (Colby & Ortman, 2014).

## THE POTENTIAL IMPACT ON LONG-TERM CARE

*10,000 Americans will turn 65 every day from now until 2029* (Kane, 2013). This is a truly staggering statistic, and its impact on the long-term care industry is almost immeasurable. What's more, certain characteristics unique to this baby boom generation will potentially intensify the impact.

## DIMINISHED HEALTH

Life expectancy in the U.S. has increased dramatically over the last century. Studies indicate, however, that the baby boom generation is not as healthy as their parent's generation (Barr, 2014). While the good news is that they will live longer than their parents, the bad news is that they suffer to a much greater degree from chronic diseases like diabetes, heart disease, obesity, and Alzheimer's. Between 2000 and 2030 the number of Americans with chronic conditions will approach 46 million, an increase of 37% (Barr, 2014). This combination of increased longevity and more chronic disease makes the burden on long-term care only heavier.

"The reality is most elderly people do not have one disease on their death certificates," says Daniel Perry, president of the Alliance for Aging Research. Multiple conditions usually require care from more than one specialist in addition to a primary care physician, and the system currently is set up in a way that doesn't encourage coordination and collaboration. "We don't have a health care system that is well-designed to diagnose, assess, prevent, postpone and treat the multiple chronic conditions that accompany the aging process," Perry says (Barr, 2014).

## FIGURE # 6:

### BOOMER HEALTH WOES
### The Average American over the age of 65 Suffers from Multiple Chronic Conditions, including:

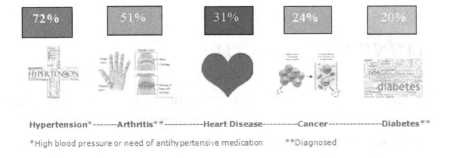

Hypertension*-------Arthritis**------------Heart Disease----------Cancer--------------Diabetes**

*High blood pressure or need of antihypertensive medication    **Diagnosed

DATA SOURCE: huffingtonpost.com. January 19, 2015, *How the Baby Boomer Generation Is Changing the U.S. Healthcare System*, Updated: 08/05/2013 5:12 am EDT

## *ALZHEIMER'S DISEASE*

The Alzheimer's Association estimates that 5.2 million Americans had Alzheimer's disease in 2014. There is no cure for Alzheimer's and no treatment that appears to stop its spread in the brain (Reid, 2015). Since Alzheimer's is slow to progress, the disease can linger for years, or decades in some cases, making the cost for both government insurance programs and for families extremely high. Alzheimer's currently costs the United States $214 billion annually. Medicare and Medicaid will spend $150 million while the remaining costs will fall largely on patients and their families (Reid, 2015). "This ***most expensive disease in America*** is devouring federal and state health care budgets and depleting the life savings of millions of victims and their families. Recent studies show that the cost of caring for Americans with Alzheimer's disease and other dementias has surpassed the cost of treatment for cancer patients or victims of heart disease, and these costs are virtually certain to go up," says T.R. Reid in a recent AARP report. While the deaths from some cancers and heart disease are declining, the number of Alzheimer's cases continues to increase every year as the population grows older (Reid, 2015).

Adding Alzheimer's disease to the already extensive list of chronic illness that inflicts the baby boomers pushes the ability of long-term care to cope almost to the limit. To make matters worse for long-term care, the enormous population spike of the baby boom generation is exacerbated by the state of the generation's health. Put simply, many more elderly people will live longer, but they will be plagued by chronic disease.

## *LIMITED FINANCIAL RESOURCES*

## **Personal Net Worth**

As the cost of long-term care increases, the ability of the baby boom generation to pay for care is decreasing. Except for the wealthiest 10 percent of the generation, boomers' financial resources shriveled following the downturn in the economy. "Middle and lower income baby boomers were absolutely decimated in the last decade, reports Ian Morrison, author, consultant and futurist. "They lost their jobs, have been unemployed, and spent down savings." In 2010, at the height of the Great Recession, the median household income for Americans 65 and older was only $31, 408 (Barr, 2013).

The Pew Charitable Trusts estimates that boomers born between 1946 and 1955 lost 28 percent of median net worth during the Great Recession, while boomers born after that lost 25 percent of median net worth. That put the two groups' median net worth at $173,000 and $111,000, respectively. At the same time, Fidelity Investments recently estimated that the total out-of-pocket medical costs for a couple retiring in 2013 will be $220,000 (Barr, 2013).

## Long-Term Care Insurance

Currently there are roughly 7.7 million LTCI policies in force in the United States; only 12.4% of adults aged 65 and older hold LTCI policies (Frank, 2012). While there is wide variation in the detailed benefits, the median benefit in the U.S. involves three years of coverage at a maximum benefit level of $150 per day. Underwriting for LTCI policies is restrictive, and it is unlikely that as the boomers age they will be able to purchase this type of coverage (Frank, 2012).

## Medicaid

Financing institutional-based care for 1.6 million older persons is a problem today. It is painfully clear that current financing strategies and the current system of long-term care delivery will not be adequate for the approximately 8 million severely disabled older persons projected to need care in 2040 (Harris-Krojetin et al, 2013).

Medicaid is by far the largest public payer for long-term care services (LTC Insurance Statistics, 2014). Few people understand, however, that Medicaid is a means-tested program that only pays health care costs for poor and disabled people (Frank, 2012).

The current long-term care system has used a mixed approach, relying first on the individual and then, following depletion of resources, the Medicaid program. Older low-income adults with functional impairments and those who incur expenses so high that they are considered medically needy are eligible to participate in Medicaid. This "all or nothing" system of support for institutional care, which requires individuals to spend almost all of their resources before governments' responsibility begins, ensures that many older people will live their final years as dependents of the state. (Harris-Krojetin et al, 2013).

## INADEQUATE FACILITIES

The 15,700 nursing homes in the country provide a total of 1,699,100 certified beds. The 22,200 residential care communities provide 851,400 licensed beds. Each day in 2012 there were 1,383,700 residents in nursing homes and 713,300 residents in residential care communities (Harris-Kojetin et al, 2013).

There are currently only enough nursing home beds in the United States to accommodate roughly 52% of the severely disabled older population. If we simply continue current nursing-home utilization ratios, we would need about 2.8 million nursing home beds by the year 2020, and 4.4 million by 2040 (SCAN, 2012).

In 2014, the senior housing annual inventory growth rate was only 1.4% (Harris-Krojetin et al, 2013). In the top 100 metropolitan markets there were only 21, 462 beds under construction (Harris-Krojetin et al, 2013). At this rate of growth we will add a total of only 107,310 beds over the next five years. However, we need 1.1 million additional beds to reach the estimated 2.8 million beds needed in 2020 (Applebaum et al, 1991). We are facing an immediate shortfall of 1 million beds over the next five years.

These numbers are staggering. It is clear that an incremental response to housing the retiring baby boomer generation will be drastically inadequate.

## CRITICAL STAFFING SHORTAGE

The professional and paraprofessional staffing shortage in long-term care discussed in Chapter One is fraught with irony. A large percentage of experienced personnel working in long-term care are the retiring baby boomers themselves, and they are not being replaced by the younger generation. The staff is rapidly becoming the patient.

Both nursing homes and home health providers have identified difficulties in the recruitment and retention of replacement personnel. Because personal care assistance dominates the long-term care needs of the chronically disabled person, staffing challenges have serious implications for both quality and cost of care (Applebaum et al, 1991).

Paraprofessional careers in LTC, such as CNAs and home health aides, are undervalued and underpaid in our society, and these workers often feel unappreciated by their employers. A major cause for the lack of respect in this field is ageism (discrimination against the elderly). Negative ageist attitudes of LTC environments "translates into non-competitive compensation and benefits for all staff categories in the clinical and managerial arenas" and unequal pay in the health care field. Ageism in the larger culture creates a tendency to equate long-term care with nursing homes, a setting older people want to avoid. In addition, sensational stories in the media about fires, abuse, and scandal bias the public's view (Rill, 2012).

Paraprofessional workers report a number of on-the-job frustrations as well: a lack of control over rules, staffing shortages, poor training, hard-to-care-for clients, and unsafe working conditions (Rill, 2012).

In a service economy with increasing competition for skilled workers, long-term care employers must provide an appealing work setting for paraprofessional workers. They must enhance several aspects of work life, including wages and benefits, working conditions, the nature of the work, status of the job, ability to advance, opportunity for other jobs, and the intrinsic value of performing the work task (Applebaum et al, 1991).

The professional and administrative staffing outlook is equally dismal. Fewer medical school students are choosing Geriatrics, and studies show that long-term care plays a minor role in the curriculum for most university programs in health administration (SPAN, 2013).

As patient enrollment is exploding, long-term care employment is becoming less attractive to both professional and paraprofessional staff. Long-term care staffing is trending toward a critical intersection.

*"I've woken up in trees, I've woken up almost hanging off cliffs, but I've always known how to sort myself out."*

*~Jack Nicholson*

# CHAPTER THREE

## Long Term Care — How Did We Get Here?

The term "long-term care" refers to services and supports to help frail older adults and younger persons with disabilities maintain their daily lives. Even today, most long-term care is provided by the families of the elderly and infirm. For thousands of years the aged have turned over the family's assets to the next generation and simply tried to stay out of the way as much as possible as family life continued.

Before the nineteenth century, no age-restricted institutions existed for long-term care. Rather, elderly individuals who needed shelter because of incapacity, impoverishment, or family isolation often ended their days in an almshouse. Placed alongside the insane, the inebriated, or the homeless, they were simply categorized as part of the community's most needy recipients. (FATE, 2013)

### *The Alms House*

In 1823, The Indigent Widows' and Single Women's Society, one of the nation's earliest old age homes, was organized in Philadelphia to "preserve many who once lived respectfully from becoming residents of the Alms House." In 1850, Boston's Home for Aged Women was founded as a haven for those who were "bone of our bone, and flesh of our flesh." Although designed for those without substantial familial support, these early homes still generally required substantial entrance fees and certificates of good character. (FATE, 2013)

As a result, for the most impoverished individuals, the almshouse still served as the last refuge in their old age. Throughout the nineteenth century, the almshouse continued to play an important part in the long-term care of the old. In fact, elderly persons became the dominant almshouse residents. (FATE, 2013)

## *The Passage of Medicare and Medicaid*

It is shocking to learn that it wasn't until the 1950s that Congress amended Social Security to allow federal support to individuals in public facilities, and the almshouse began to disappear from the elderly care landscape. In 1965, the passage of Medicare and Medicaid provided additional impetus to the growth of the modern nursing-home industry.

Early investigations of this new industry in the 1970s, however, revealed that these institutions were providing substandard care. They were labeled "warehouses" for the old. Beginning in 1971, therefore, policymakers began to enact numerous government regulations to control the quality of long-term care and the modern nursing home industry began to emerge. By 2000, nursing homes had become a 100 billion dollar industry, paid largely by Medicaid.

## The Modern Day Ad hoc System of Long Term Care

The present day ad hoc system of long-term care is a recent phenomenon. The evolution from the almshouse to high end residential care communities that combine independent living, assisted living, and nursing homes all on one campus, has taken only 60 years. During this period, small private group homes and assisted living facilities also began popping up when it became apparent that the elderly didn't all need the same level of care.

The greater majority of long-term care for the elderly is still provided by families in the home, but this delivery of long-term care presents major challenges and costs for the family. Spouses and adult children combined provide approximately 80% of the daily care received by older adults. 75% of these family caregivers are women and these women often find themselves in precarious financial and health situations. This traditional arrangement is starting to evaporate with societal shifts in the role of women as they seek careers outside the home. Not only is the self-image of women changing, but the need for two incomes is driving women back into the workforce as well. (Johnson et al, 2007)

At the same time that the traditional supply of home based caregivers is shrinking, the Great Recession of 2008 has virtually put a stop to the construction of institutional long-term care facilities. Already in short supply, residential care facilities for the baby boom generation of retirees will be woefully inadequate, if not entirely nonexistent.

Although there are a number of delivery system issues that arise when thinking about providing long-term care in the future, this combined shortage of home based care and institutional facilities poses the most fundamental questions on the nature of the service delivery system itself. For example, what does adequate long-term care assistance to those in need actually look like? Do we provide care primarily in institutional or community settings? And how is this balance determined?

## Can the Current System and Infrastructure be Maintained?

Although the answers to these questions are not clear-cut, it is obvious that such issues need to be addressed prior to the tremendous expansion of the population expected to experience long-term care needs. Providing institutional-based care for 1.3 million older persons is a problem today. It is painfully clear that the current system of long-term care delivery will not be adequate for the approximately 8 million severely disabled older persons projected to need care in 2040. As the number of older people in need of long-term care doubles and then triples, and possibly quadruples, the development of a coherent system of care will be essential. (Johnson et al, 2007)

If there are no long-term care facilities available to the baby boomers, they will have to remain at home. Who will care for them? Current providers of long-term care are already discussing a growing service delivery problem: a shortage in the supply of paraprofessional workers. Home health care providers have identified difficulties in the recruitment and retention of those individuals responsible for providing the personal care to those with long-term care needs. Poor reputation and job image, inadequate training, low pay, little chance for advancement, and unsafe working conditions all conspire to make home health care positions unattractive and unstable.

Finally, continually escalating long-term care costs have placed the ideological issue of who should be responsible for the elderly with chronic disabilities at the heart of the debate. Is ensuring that each individual has proper long-term care an individual's responsibility or is it the responsibility of government? Neither can afford the expense. Where will the money come from?

As the baby boom generation retires at the rate of 3 million per year for the next 20 years, the long-term care industry stands wide-eyed and stunned. "Where will we put all these old people? Who will care for them? Who is going to pay for all this?"

*"Not a speck of light is showing/So the danger must be growing... Are the fires of Hell a-glowing? / Is the grisly Reaper mowing? / Yes! The danger must be growing – 'cause the rowers keep on rowing... and they're certainly not showing any sign that they are slowing!"*

*~Willy Wonka*

# CHAPTER FOUR

## Is it Time to Panic?

### *Do We Have Time to Plan and React?*

It is apparent that neither the government, nor the nation as a whole, will be able to come up with a solution to the massive retirement bubble represented by the baby boom generation. The sheer size of the problem overwhelms our ability to plan and react to the housing, staffing, and financing shortfall that is about to swamp the nation's long-term caregivers. Continuing to simply build more traditional nursing homes and assisted living facilities; to hire more low-paid and uneducated workers to care for the elderly; to expect Medicaid to pay for millions of additional chronically ill elderly patients; to rely on the eldest daughter to forsake her career to care for her retired parents; to hope that the baby boomers will not need as much care because of their healthy lifestyle is to remain in denial and drown in the *Tidal Wave* that is washing over our society.

## *Hope is on the Horizon*

However, despite much of the gloominess surrounding the aging of the baby boom generation, there are reasons to be optimistic. Since its inception, the United States has defined itself as an innovative nation. From science and technology to the arts, a dynamic interaction of ideas, traditions, and talents has fueled new achievements and influenced the national experience.

Long-term care professionals are currently developing innovative care models combined with advances in technology that could save the system billions even as baby boomers pour into Medicare and live longer (Barr, 2014).

The Affordable Care Act has become a major driver of innovation in improving care for older patients (Leopardo, 2013). The Medicare program is promoting and testing models that reward the value rather than the volume of care delivered; if effective, they should make caring for the boomers more efficient and relieve stress on the system. Projects backed by the Centers for Medicare & Medicaid Services through the ACA include efforts to test bundled payment for acute care and post-acute care stays, the use of community-based organizations to assist patients in the transition out of the hospital, the creation of accountable-care organizations, and the use of patient-centered medical homes (Barr, 2014).

Innovation in facility design and mobile health also holds promise for improving the quality and effectiveness of care (Barr, 2014). Specialized acute-care for the elderly units in hospitals and resident facilities that offer a spectrum of medical assistance are becoming more common.

Mobile health offers a way to replace or enhance office-based care, such as by monitoring medical status or telling patients to take a medication. Patients are getting more adept at such things as monitoring and checking their blood sugar levels (Barr, 2014).

In an ideal world, the new, more-efficient care models, the improvements in technology, and the care itself will increase supply capacity enough to offset the extra demand created by the boomers.

Continued creative innovation is the answer. To formulate a successful strategy, leaders need to change the way they look at the future.

> *"The supreme art of war is to*
> *subdue the enemy without fighting.*
> *The greatest victory is that which*
> *requires no battle."*
>
> *~Sun Tzu, The Art of War*

# CHAPTER FIVE

## A Pre-emptive Strike Through Creative Innovation?

### First-Steps

The following creative suggestions come from discussions with industry leaders. We present them here as food for creative thought, not as a panacea for the problems facing long-term care in the 21st century.

### Facilities

The seeds of a solution to the elderly housing problem are planted locally. Since the most valuable asset that the baby boom generation has accumulated over the past fifty years is their home, this asset could be utilized to revive the concept of the small neighborhood group home.

In this possible scenario, one of a small group of five or six retirees retains ownership of their home, while the others sell their homes and move in with him/her. The resident who owns the home lives rent-free and enjoys the financial assistance of the other residents. The group could then afford to hire one full-time equivalent home health aide to look after the needs of the entire group.

In other words, whittle down the impending baby boom long-term care housing shortage, one neighborhood at a time, rather than thinking of it as a problem that the younger generation must solve for the baby boom generation.

This first-step concept challenges the traditional thinking that government takes responsibility for all social problems. It recognizes the reality that it is too late for the government to provide the additional beds necessary to accommodate retiring baby boomers. It suggests that baby boomers themselves look at housing already in their possession and find a way to utilize it for their own benefit.

If only one local social worker could organize the first neighborhood small group home along these lines, the country could be off and running in an entirely new direction.

## *Finance*

At the end of 2013 there was 19.5 trillion dollars of life insurance and annuities in force in the United States. This enormous financial asset lies dormant waiting to cover funeral expenses and enrich the next generation. We might consider converting all life insurance to long-term care insurance.

The program might be administered by the underwriters along the lines of a reverse mortgage. This would free up a substantial asset for the long-term care of the baby boom generation and avoid the projected insolvency of Medicaid.

This would require a new line of thinking on the part of both the insured and the insurer. Again, the program requires a creative first-step. However, when combined with the small group home concept above, a new horizon begins to emerge.

## *Staffing*

President Obama, in his State of the Union address, suggested that the country consider providing a free community college education for all qualified applicants. The long-term care paraprofessional is the first position that should be considered in conjunction with new direction in education.

A Community College program could upgrade the position of Home Health Aide to a professional position by requiring community college training and certification of all long-term care paraprofessionals.

Paraprofessionals might expand their skills to the proper administration of medication, for example, and relieve pressure on the RN profession in long-term care.

After graduation and certification, long-term care workers would be compensated as professionals and have a chance at further education and advancement.

## *Technology*

The greatest leap forward in efficiency of care has been provided by specific technological innovation. Over the last 20 years, through the power of the Internet and the development of highly efficient software systems — agencies have been able to collect and mine critical data on their clients that has, in turn, empowered them to deliver better care.

Information technology systems focused on helping professionals deliver and track services has revolutionized how agencies manage cases. Case management software systems are helping home health aide workers and long-term care facilities achieve better results.

It is in this area that we would like to take a deeper dive and lay out a plan for those agencies to use as a benchmark for measurement against their current technology and as a roadmap to consider when searching for new technology.

*"Not everything that can be counted counts, and not everything that counts can be counted."*

*~Albert Einstein, Physicist*

# CHAPTER SIX

## Changing the Paradigm Through Technology

As demonstrated in this book — a perfect storm is looming. However, there is hope. Long-term care professionals are currently developing innovative care models combined with advances in technology that could save the system billions even as baby boomers pour into Medicare and live longer (Barr, 2014).

But — as we've seen over the last 8 years, agencies that serve families and children are experiencing significant increases in demand for their services. Unfortunately, as the expectations and burdens have increased, funding has not kept pace. In fact, in many cases, budgets have actually decreased.

For many of those on the frontlines, helping others, these factors have led to an overwhelming cycle: Caseworkers are suffering from the pressures of having too many cases and too many records to keep track of. In some circumstances, mounting caseloads have led to poor morale or even burnout.

Of course, those who can suffer the most from an overwhelmed system are those who can least afford it. These unfortunates are the clients you serve. Two recent independent surveys from Michigan and New Jersey confirm that non-profits are being challenged as never before. In each survey more than 60% reported a significant increase in demand (in one survey it was as high as 73%). But half of the respondents report that they are unable to fully meet the demand for their service.

## More Staff or More Efficiency?

So as demand increases, one solution is to add more staff. This will ease the burden on the current caseworkers and make sure that your clients are served adequately. The one problem with this solution is that it often is not realistic. The budget may not be there to add more staff.

## Working Harder or Smarter?

Another solution is to get your staff to work harder. In the world of non-profits, this is also not realistic. You already have people working harder for less money than they would likely receive in the for-profit sector. And as your staff takes on more burdens, morale can dip, thus making it even more difficult to increase performance.

There is one other solution . . . work smarter. Your entire organization can get the necessary tools to increase efficiency. Here is a key point about better tools and processes: they have a 'snowball' effect that improves performance and morale in all areas. This section is dedicated to the proposition that an affordable, case management software system is the quickest and best way to increase the quality of your services.

Already using a system? Excellent! Use this section as a benchmark for re-evaluation. If the system is giving you what you need — you're ahead of the game. Consider yourself part of the 15% of agencies that have a good understanding of the information foundation that you need to help prepare for the next five years. But is information, alone, enough? Could you benefit from improved process workflow or better reporting? More on that in a bit.

On the other hand — if you're among the remaining 85% of professionals who have not optimized their case management and data reporting processes and who are suffering from data constraints or inefficiencies — we hope to outline a clear path. Whether you're currently using a paper file and folder system or struggling with a software system that falls short, there are options that can get the job done for far less than you might expect.

## *Leveraging Good Software and a Case Management System*

When was the last time you looked for a software solution? The Internet has made it easy for us to type in a few search words or phrases into a search engine and immediately retrieve 10 viable options that match our keywords. Today, the truth is that there are a lot of case management choices available, many of which have popped up over the last few years. Unfortunately, a lot of them are just not really any good. If you've been tasked with finding a solution that can help your agency — then this next section should be useful to you.

WELCOME TO THE AGING TIDAL WAVE

*"Faith is taking the first step even when you don't see the whole staircase."*

*~Martin Luther King, Jr.*

# CHAPTER SEVEN

## Three Steps to Outlining the Perfect Case Management System

### *Three Steps to Outlining the Perfect Case Management System*

Because you have to manage so much to keep your agency running, taking time to sort through the best options can seem overwhelming. For this reason, we've outlined and combined together a simple **three-step process** to remove the confusion. You'll also find resources and worksheets in the Bonus chapter of this book that you can print and fill out to help you put these steps into practical action.

### *Step 1* — *Asking the Right Questions*

The worst thing you can do when considering adding or upgrading ANY software is to jump in before asking enough questions. Many agencies put off adding a new software solution because they think they will have to abandon current forms, procedures, and workflow . . . and they are not sure they want to do that. For many, "Change" is not easy. For some, new software and technology can be confusing. Let's face it, new technology can be scary.

In short, what most agencies really want to know is this: "Will case management software end up being more disruptive than helpful?" The answer: good software is infinitely more helpful then disruptive. But that is a general answer. What leaders need are detailed responses that help them come to a well-thought out decision.

Below are some of the more common questions about case management software. This might not cover every question you have, but this can serve as a good start and foundation to your exploration.

*A quick disclaimer: the answers below apply to good case management software solutions. Just like any other product or service, not all of the options are created equal. As you examine your possibilities, make sure you ask these questions about any solution you are analyzing.*

1. **Can our current forms be used or will we have to start from scratch?**

   You should be able to add and integrate forms into the software. Any software worth investing in will allow for this type of customization. But what is key to understand is that software should allow you to go beyond just adding current forms. New software can be a spur to making your forms and workflow more responsive and efficient. In short, you can add your current forms, but you can also benefit by modifying them where it makes sense.

## 2. Will we be able to add forms we want to create as our needs evolve?

To give an example from our own software, there is a powerful and innovative module available called Pathways. Pathways has many benefits, including the ability to track meetings, documents, and events. Pathways also has a robust form creation tool that allows you to generate new data collection forms and assessments to meet your needs. This is just one example from our software. The key is to ask these "functionality" questions now and find out what the software can do before you invest in it. Does the solution you're pursuing allow you to add new content, forms and information gathering tools easily?

## 3. We have some specific reporting rules and requirements we need to follow. Can these be incorporated?

Customizable reports should be easy to set-up one time and then be run anytime they are needed. If you're reporting rules require a specific documentation of client interactions, this can also be set-up. If you have specific reporting requirements, the ability to track all of this and KNOW that it is being done right is one of the biggest benefits of the right software solution.

4. **We are closely tied to other organizations and need to interact with them efficiently (data collection, sharing, etc.). Can our software "talk" to their software?**

In place of cumbersome emailing of spreadsheets or other antiquated methods of data sharing, web-based applications allow for efficient exchange of data between systems. Since there can be exceptions depending on the type of software being used by your partners, it is a good idea to ask about your specific situation during a consultation. Even when automatic data sharing is not possible, other simple solutions for reporting data can usually be implemented.

5. **We already use a software system — it is just not very good. But we need the data from the old system to carry over without having to re-enter everything. How does that work?**

Data imports from spreadsheets, other databases, or legacy systems are relatively simple in most cases — with the right software tools and team. This is another case where a consultation with a qualified software development company will provide a more specific answer, but in general, importing crucial data to your new system is perfectly manageable.

6. **A big stumbling block to our progress has been the inability to slice and dice data to measure the right things.**

As a matter of fact, this is one of the areas that many organizations underrate, at first, and then end up relying on heavily. One of the keys here is the "real-time" access to data. In many cases, agencies have the data they need to make good decisions and adjustments. However, it is buried and not brought to the surface until it is too late to be useable. This is a case where software can be a "double win" when it comes to data:

    a.  The data can be sliced up and delivered in the way that is most useful, and;

    b.  It will be available on command, so it can be used for real-time decision-making.

**7. We are worried that this will be overly complicated and basically turn into a technical "boondoggle." How difficult will this be to implement?**

This is a real concern. It is always a good idea to get a demonstration of any software you are considering. But it is also important to ask deeper questions. Find out how much support you will receive — particularly during the first few weeks of implementation. These crucial first weeks are the most important time for success. Personalized coaching during this time is very beneficial.

**8. Isn't the investment in good software out of reach for small to medium non-profits?**

Not too long ago, this might have been true. With the advent of cloud computing solutions, this is simply no longer the case. To be blunt, any software company that is still selling high-priced solutions is behind the times. There are now affordable options well within reach of small and medium sized organizations.

## *Step 2:* *Focus Areas | How to Thoroughly Analyzing Your Current Case Management Process*

Step 1 gave you a thorough understanding of where you are now. Step 2 is all about where you can go. There are ten key aspects of this step. Remember, as you read through this list — it's important to keep in mind the end goal here... to better serve your clients! Another key is not to set self-imposed limits before executing this step. Some organizations assume ahead of time that certain technologies are automatically outside their reach because it will be beyond their budget.

Now, of course, the budget will eventually enter into any decision made. But this step is about the ideal solution for your organization, so you should avoid limiting yourself right from the start.

*Here are some questions and thoughts to help you:*

To make solid decisions on how to improve, you first need to get a clear picture of where your organization currently stands. What follows are areas of focus for optimizing case management.

*(Note: the "Current Case Management Worksheet" at the back of this book contains questions for each area and has space for answers. It is recommended that you finish reading this book first and then revisit this section again later to print and complete the worksheet).*

# Focus Area #1 – Standardization

Would a standardized formatting for all or some of your forms and documents improve your process? A software solution can provide a powerful and efficient way to make sure that all forms are filled out consistently and that no required information is omitted. It is important to think through how this could best work for your organization.

# Focus Area #2 – Scalability

If you expect that your organization will grow over time, it only makes sense to find a case management software system that can grow with it – failure to do so now will mean big headaches later. Let's consider the both ends of the spectrum . . . a pilot vs. a full-blown enterprise system. Starting a pilot case management program allows you to build in and test functionality with a small "champion" group who can work out any "kinks" in your foundation before you look to "grow" your system. Beyond the pilot program, you may look to add other users – or in the case of a system for a larger organization such as a city, county or state-level agency, adding other departments or teams of stakeholders. The kind of software that can rise to meet these future needs is said to be scalable.

Let's dig into the details of what scalability is, and why it's important for your agency. In practice, scalability can get complex and technical. But at the root it is actually a very simple concept. It has two basic components: 1) your needs right now, and, 2) what you will need in the future.

You can think of the first part of scalability — your current needs — as the "Goldilocks and the Three Bears" problem.

You don't want your software to be "too big" because that will mean you will be paying for more than you need. You don't want your software to be "too small" because then it will not have the capacity to do what you need it to do.

You need your software to be "just right." It needs to be powerful enough to meet the current and future capacities of your agency, but not so large that you pay for much more than you need.

But that is only the first part of scalability. To talk about the second part, we need to take the Goldilocks story one step further:

## A Twist to the Story

In our version of the story, Goldilocks grows up. The software that is "just right" now might be way too small in 5 years. And this is the whole key to scalability: It is the ability to grow with your agency so you don't have to make radical changes to your software as you increase the capacity of your organization. Many agencies have found out, too late, that they should have picked a scalable software system sooner and then they suffer through the pain and expense of fixing the problem.

Choosing a software application that is scalable means this problem melts away. You can have seamless upgrades and increased capacity on the case management system you and your staff will have already learned. You will not have to re-invent the software wheel every time you grow to serve more clients.

## Cloud Computing: Why Scalable Software is So Much More Affordable Now

Up until very recently, one of the biggest roadblocks to high-performing software was price. No matter how good and innovative the software company was, there was no way around the cost issue. That has all changed with cloud-based technology.

Unfortunately, many software companies that serve agencies HAVE NOT made the switch to this new technology. Without using the latest innovations, it is still the same old choice between performance and price.

But software companies that HAVE made the switch to cloud-based systems can now offer agencies very specific solutions. Software that used to be available only to the biggest agencies is now realistic for small to medium-sized organizations (including 5-20 person non-profits).

The power of this goes beyond affordability. With cloud technology, scaling up to meet the needs of larger non-profits is much easier. So when the agency with the staff of 20 grows to 100+, the software can grow right alongside.

It also means that larger agencies can get exactly what they need right now. Are you starting to see the power of scalability, especially when tied to cloud computing technology? It is an excellent time to be considering your software options.

## Focus Area #3 – Collaboration

What would be ideal in terms of access to case management files for your agency? This is a key area to focus on. Some organizations have lived so long with their data trapped in multiple, hard-to-access containers that they have trouble imagining the morale boost and service efficiencies that can come with crucial data being available easily to those who are authorized to view it.

Many "community of care" models would fail without a

process for collaboration. The right software allows for sharing of information.

Many organizations have found ways to greatly increase collaboration through more robust access to client case management. This step is the time to brainstorm ways that your own collaboration could improve with a better system.

## Focus Area #4 – Intake Process

For many agencies, there are specific documents that absolutely MUST be completed before a prospective client can be assisted. What system do you currently have in place to standardize and track all the clients when they come to you for services?

Ask yourself whether your system is highly manual. Is it heavy on handwritten forms and file folders? If it is, standardization can be a problem. Paper means that caseworkers and clients can often miss filling in crucial information, or do it incorrectly. More stringent auditing and training is sometimes necessary when using paper systems in order to get everyone on the same page.

Paper systems also raise issues of tracking and access. With paper systems, if certain key forms are accidently skipped, there is often no easy way to catch the error. If multiple people need access to the original intake forms, manual systems are the least efficient and frustrating for your staff.

If you use a computer-based system, ask yourself how well it meshes with your intake process. Many agencies struggle with older, legacy systems. These systems often provide no product updates and become more out-dated each passing year. Often with older systems, technical support is minimal to non-existent. This can lead to significant frustrations for

## Answer These Crucial Questions and Watch Your Organization Transform.

1. What data would help me reach and accomplish my current goal objectives faster?

2. What do my clients and their families expect to find or achieve with my programs and services?

3. What knowledge do I need to reach my next goal easier and more certain?

4. What is my current expectation of a positive outcome and how do I measure that?

5. What do I need to learn about my client situations to make better decisions for their needs?

6. What do I need to learn about my caseworkers to allow them to be more productive?

7. What administrative duties could be automated allowing me to re-focus my efforts into improving assessments of family situations and increasing the efficiency of elderly care and adult protection?

both caseworkers and clients during the intake process.

Another key area to analyze is the amount of time it takes to complete your intake process. To get a true picture, you should factor in time spent tracking down missing documents, computer downtime, and filing time.

Oftentimes, for some home health aides , paperwork isn't correlated or entered into a system until days later, when they're back in their offices. A good idea, when analyzing, is to sit down with your caseworkers and ask them what frustrates them about the intake process. A best practice is to ask them to be specific about what eats up their time as they on-board clients.

A good thing to remember when looking for a new system is that the good ones are now web-based and can be accessible from anywhere with an Internet connection, including mobile-ready smart phones and tablets like the iPhone and iPad.

# Focus Area 5: Workflow, Reporting and Tracking

## Workflow

Do you have a typical process that the majority of your clients follow as they receive your services? Even if you don't have one you can call typical, it is likely you can think through some typical types of experiences in delivering services to your clients.

Once you sketch out some typical interactions, it is time to think through the 'touch-points' with your case management system. In a typical situation, after the intake process, when is the next point that a caseworker will need to refer to (or add to) the client's file or documentation?

It can be very helpful to outline each step specifically and look at the process and whether it is allowing you to serve your clients in the best way possible. The worksheets at the end of this report will help you dig into the details. For instance, one crucial area is how data about your clients moves with your organization's workflow. How many people in your organization typically access a single client's data? Do all the staff members who need access to complete client information actually get what they need, simply and efficiently?

Many organizations are plagued with problems involving

**An Example of One Agency's Quest to Fix Their Incident Reporting Process.**

For years, an agency in St. Louis, MO struggled with how they managed incident reporting. Essentially, the process was like this: when an incident occurred, it required a caseworker to fill out a written report and then, through a series of steps, obtain approval from various stakeholders (who were located in different offices, sometimes off campus) before the processing was complete. Each time they sought the next level of "sign off," the incident report would be physically pulled out of one person's bin and moved over to the next person in the approval "chain." The approval time typically took a week.

After finding a good software system, the agency was able to transform this process by making the incident "reporting" electronic, collaborative and most importantly, web-based. They were able to create a streamlined workflow that guided the process and dramatically cut the processing time. The new process is now as follows: caseworker completes the incident report, checks a box for approval authority — which automatically sends an email to the first supervisor in the list for review and sign off. When the supervisor approves it, the report automatically goes to the second supervisor for sign off, etc., and in the process is 100% secure. At no time is the report "sitting" in a box where it private data could be compromised. Instead, when a supervisor is notified, they are required to log into the system to actually see and approve the report.

Now, a process that took 4-5 days to complete can now be done the same day — and at times in just a matter of minutes. That's workflow.

sharing data. If you find that crucial information is trapped inside of different 'data silos', note this in your case management analysis. Also, how important are automated alerts, triggers and notifications that can be fired off to a caseworker alerting them of overdue or upcoming tasks?

## *Modules and Dashboard*

Do you have certain areas where being handed a well organized, easy-to-use solution would be a welcomed relief?

In other words, how would you like a turnkey solution that takes the pressure off you and simplifies a task, your job or even your day? Maybe a module to handle billing or grant management? We know you're busy — so possibly one or two workflow tools that help you stay on track?

There are a lot of options available, so think about what areas need the most help. Also, what kind of information would be most helpful to your caseworkers in staying on top of their cases? If they logged into a main screen (or 'dashboard'), what alerts, notifications, reminders, etc. would be most helpful in keeping track of their clients?

## Reporting

Another area to analyze: the ability of your current case management system to track and report crucial information that keeps you out of legal or other difficulties. Unfortunately, everyone has heard of the tragedies that can occur when clients slip through the safety net provided by social services. Excellent case management processes significantly lessen the chances of this occurring.

Worst-case scenarios aside, what are the costs of less-than-optimal case management for the day-to-day quality you deliver to all your clients? As you analyze your case management system, play devil's advocate and ask what is going wrong or could go wrong with how you currently manage cases. These are not always the most pleasant questions to put to your organization. But it is better to do it now. It will be much more painful to go through after a poor, or even disastrous, client outcome.

## Reporting Constraints

Many organizations are seriously constrained by the lack of information they have — about how their clients are responding to their programs and services. The transformation occurs when you begin to realize that we now operate in a hyper-connected world where trends change direction instantly, and only knowing precisely how your clients are responding to you consistently can help you make sure you're not going in the wrong direction.

Sadly, this seems to be one of the truths that many human service organizations ignore, and they don't put enough attention towards (or are unsure how to maximize) their data and information. All too often, it costs them far more than they realize.

### *How to measure*

Put simply, their constraint is that they don't have the right tools in place to really know how their strategy and execution is working in the real world. And that makes it impossible for them to leverage their success or to cut unproductive strategies short before they break the bank — and more importantly — before they put a child or client at major risk.

The good news is that the right case management software makes it easy to instantly identify changes in how your programs are affecting your clients or patients. When used correctly, the real-time intelligence you receive from a system can transform how you receive your data — which is the key to improving the outcomes for your clients.

There are affordable software options that provide the ability to slice and collate data in very dynamic and effective ways. The reporting tools now available can measure progress, note areas where your organization is weak, and track outcomes. The incredible potency of data management and reporting tools allows you to spot troubling trends very fast and design a response. These types of solutions are simply not possible with paper and file systems or out-dated software systems.

### *What to do with what you learn:*

By telling you more about your clients and the services you provide, you'll have all the information needed for program administration, risk management, planning evaluation, budgeting and continued funding.

Many times, grant applications and other important sources of funding hinge upon being able to precisely measure and report data and outcomes. What data and report capabilities would improve your chances to obtain more funding?

In today's rapidly changing business environment, the watchword is "constant vigilance" — watching your metrics (like a hawk), monitoring and adapting your client care plans and treatment plans ON THE FLY and daily (if necessary) to ensure that it continues to fit YOUR VISION, hand-in-glove.

"We have different people that serve different roles at our agency. Depending on their job function — certain people only need access to certain areas of the system. I've worked with other software platforms where security setup was a difficult thing to manage and maintain. What security considerations must be researched and met before we ever make a decision on a new system?"

## Focus Area 6: Information Security

Your information needs to be protected. EXCEL and other similar desktop tools aren't robust enough to protect your data correctly, and relying on them is risky. Information is your lifeblood. If it's wrong or compromised you're done. The implications can be catastrophic. Data can get into the wrong hands or major funding decisions can be skewed because of bad information — both of which can close down your operation. Who benefits then?

Security controls must also be easy to use and configure. In so many cases with software — the security controls are cumbersome, inflexible and not configurable by the end user or administrator of the software system.

Each agency also needs to have a security plan in place that serves as the SOP when it comes to protecting client information. First and foremost — whatever system you decide to use — make sure that at the end of the day, you (and not your vendor) own your data.

**This is an Interactive Book with Free Videos, Case Studies and Other Useful Tools!**

Please register by visiting the website, register, introduce yourself, share what you do and your biggest problem that you'd like to tackle with information management.

On this site you can see free videos and an opportunity to get a free, one-hour consultation (a $150 value) with a seasoned, FAMCare specialist.

Visit: http://try.famcare.net/megaresources
or send an email to: info@globalvisiontech.com
or call: 678-965-6821

## What Should Your Information Security Plan Contain?

Following are some of the measures you should include in your maintenance plan. The integrity and security of your data server and system should include:

- Physical security
- Authentication and password security
- Antivirus software
- State of the art firewalls
- VPNs
- Logging and auditing
- Timed access control
- Software/hardware not available to the public
- Data not residing ON the web

## Ideal Set up and Parameters to Consider:

- For hosting purposes — leverage a consulting company or vendor that utilizes state-of-the-art, world-class data centers that they own and monitor or co-located data centers. Also consider a service that allows for mirroring and redundant server backup services.
- A good data center should offer a high level of security that is maintained through a five level system which is comprised of access codes, a security guard station, biometric hand scanners, electronic proximity readers and security cameras.

- Confirm that these environments are designed around industry best practices and are audited by a reputable certification company such as SAS-70 or SSAE-16 TYPE II.
- Experience counts — make sure you are working with a proven organization with seasoned professionals for managing hardware, operating systems, and applications who have at least 5+ years of experience running mission critical based applications. This experience will set your hosting apart from you hosting it yourself or with a mid-range, third party option. At the end of the day, you want to be working with an organization that can guarantee and provide an extremely secure and highly available service.
- Confirm that network connectivity access and Internet bandwidth are each covered by Service Level Agreements assuring 99.99% up time.
- Data Backups? Regular backups need to occur nightly and off-site storage should occur 1Xmonth, UPS delivered — at a bare minimum.
- Encryption — consider an application that has encryption capabilities for the most sensitive client data such as those data points covered under HIPAA — mainly PHI (protected health information). Encryption should be at the level of financial institutions or at 128 bit minimum.

GEORGE RITACCO

- Your data center and vendor need to run data availability tests to ensure that their restore processes work properly in the event a restore is needed. Taking certain precautions to ensure that the media being stored hasn't reached the end of its useful life is smart and prudent. Testing backup media on a regular basis to provide assurance that the backup media is usable, recoverable and not in conflict with any changes made to the underlying operation system and/or application, should be part of your plan.
- Leveraging state-of-the-art firewalls for intrusion prevention and having a plan for ongoing penetration testing to measure the integrity of the firewalls each month should be mission critical.
- Point and click interface that is extremely easy to learn and use will save you time, money and headaches later, and can also help to avert a data disaster!

Remember — your data is your data! Make sure it's easy to get to, extract and view. At the end of the day, you need to have an easy way to extract all of the data you type into your system, either through a series of reports or data extraction tools.

## Focus Area 7: Smart Enough for a Smart Phone?

Originally, web-based meant accessible from anywhere with

an Internet connection and a web-browser. Today, it means so much more. Mobile technology has added new dimensions to web-based technology and now entire software systems are accessible and usable from a smart phone or tablet such as the iPhone, iPad and/or the collection of Android-enabled devices. Having the ability to access and update a client or patient's record "on-the-fly" from wherever you are: at their home, your facility, the hospital, in traffic, or in court, has become absolutely necessary to make all information as real-time as possible. For example, the home health aide who needs to update the home office of a critical find discovered during a routine visit does so and, seconds later, their supervisor gets an alert and takes action. The bottom line — it is no longer necessary to wait days before you can get to your office and enter your information into your software system.

The speed and delivery of accurate and actionable information makes all the difference if your job is to protect your clients from of any life-threatening situations.

## Once and Done!

Web-based systems also follow a "once and done" philosophy. Often times, older software systems force users to enter the same information multiple times on behalf of a client — depending on the forms they use. Something as simple as a name and address is typed multiple times in order to complete data forms, whereas in a web-based system information entered once automatically flows to other areas and forms in the system —saving you time and resources.

## Software Installs and Updates

With web-based software there is nothing to install or

update. Everything is done for you automatically and there is never a need to manage a complicated install or update process. As mentioned earlier, there is also never a need for you to run backups on your data, as back-ups are done remotely from the cloud. In addition, there is no hardware to manage and/or equipment to buy and upgrade.

## Focus Area 8: Personalization & Configurability

It is highly recommended that you seek a case management software platform that works "out of the box" and is not entirely custom. The reason for this is fairly straightforward — it will save you a lot of time, money and headaches in the long run.

An "out of the box" or off-the-shelf system allows you to leverage *The Basics* — the more standardized case management processes such as: intake, progress notes, program enrollment, assessments and evaluations, discharge summaries and treatment plans. Knowing that a system has many tools available to you immediately is great, however a system that can be configured quickly and/or tailored based on your needs (whether presently or in the future) should be a big consideration.

Updating field names (changing "case" notes to "progress" notes to match your agencies vernacular) and hiding fields off existing forms (because you never ask those questions of your clients) is an important consideration. Being able to add your own data points is also important. When it's all said and done, you want to be able to make quick changes to data points, forms, case alerts and workflow as needs arise and change.

## Focus Area 9: Dynamic Scheduling

Staying on top of your staff, client and patient appointments is another critical area where a good case management system can make a big difference.

Some features you need to look for are the ability to:

- Effectively assign staff time and appointments
- Manage and track resource usage (vehicles, equipment)
- Schedule room and facility time
- Administrative assistants able to review and reassign clinician schedules, as necessary
- Ensure each client receives prompt appointment scheduling
- Create calendars for user groups or individuals

## Focus Area 10: Training & Support

For some organizations, the time and effort to get new staff competent and comfortable with handling case management documentation is a significant issue. Things to think about in this area include:

- ✓ Are you confident that all your caseworkers are proficient in managing documentation?
- ✓ How much time does it take to get caseworkers to learn new things or change processes?
- ✓ Is the training your staff receives consistent?
- ✓ What system is in place to support staff as questions arise in case management and documentation?
- ✓ What kind of outside support would be ideal for your case management system?
- ✓ If you are using a software system currently, do you have staff to deal with hardware and software issues as they arise?

✓ What would initial training on any new system look like — ideally?

The above list is a comprehensive look at what any agency should consider when thinking about a case management system. Completing the worksheets at the end of this report will allow you to explore the right solution in a comprehensive fashion.

That covers the 10 main areas of focus, but it is a good idea to think of any other areas where your case management documentation could be stronger. Once you have worked through all this, you have completed Step 2. Again, you are strongly encouraged to fill out the companion worksheets at the end of this book. Some organizations print out multiple copies of the worksheets and hold a staff meeting to go through the material. This process can uncover fresh angles and give you the best overall picture of case management strengths and weaknesses.

So, you've figured out where you are now. And you've started to get a pretty good handle on what a good solution would look like. But now what? How do you turn all this analysis into action?

# STEP 3: FIND AN EXPERT TO GUIDE YOU TO A CONCRETE SOLUTION (AND DON'T PAY FOR IT!)

Okay, if you've read this far, chances are that one of these three applies to you:

- You are on a paper and file system only, but want something better;
- You have an older software system that has become less than ideal;
- You have a newer software system that is cumbersome or plagued by technical problems.

Whichever applies to your agency, the underlying problem is the same in each case. You have something that is not working for you, is eroding staff morale, and is delivering less than your clients deserve. You've done the hard work of thinking through what you need. Now you need to invite in an expert to demonstrate possible solutions.

Global Vision Technologies (GVT) has developed a unique consulting program that allows agencies to explore case management software solutions in an environment free from pressure sales presentations. The "GVT Case Management System Assessment" is your opportunity to get your case management software questions answered without feeling obligated or pressured. We do not charge for this consulting session.

Once you've completed the worksheets at the end of this report, you've actually taken the first step in the assessment process. Although we don't require these be completed to receive your complimentary assessment, we find that the agencies that do complete them get the most out of a "GVT Case Management System Assessment." When our consultants have your worksheet answers prior to meeting with you, they can make sure all your questions and concerns are addressed.

Now, don't get us wrong — GVT does have an excellent case management system and we love to demonstrate how it has worked wonders for many agencies, directors and caseworkers. We've had many organizations smoothly transition from a paper file system to our system. We've also helped many switch from a software system that was falling short. Our solution is called "FAMCare: Rapid Case Management Software."

But is it the perfect solution for your organization? We can't give a complete and honest answer to that question without meeting with you and delivering a full assessment.

However, we can provide you with some information right now that will give you a basic idea of what FAMCare delivers and who has been successful with it.

**FAMCare is:**

**Proven:** Our first FAMCare system was launched 13 years ago and over the years we've worked with hundreds of directors, administrators, and caseworkers to refine it into a practical system that delivers results.

**Affordable:** One of the biggest barriers to high-performance software is price. With our unique, cloud-based technology, we've made the kind of quality system that used to be only available to the biggest non-profits and was not realistic for small to medium-sized organizations. (We have a lot of clients that are 5-20 person shops. Our system is flexible enough to handle that or scale up to handle much larger clients with hundreds or thousands of users).

**Personalized:** We mean this both literally and figuratively. Literally, our innovations now allow for programs to be customized to meet specific needs. But we also mean that we provide the type of personal support and training. No user of FAMCare is ever "just another account." We have added a page later in this report so you can hear what others say about us in their own words.

**What about the specific benefits of FAMCare: Rapid Case Management Software?**

✓ Data is secure and backed-up regularly
✓ Data is more visible and available
✓ World-class reporting tools and data management
✓ Client focus improves because hardware and software are not your headache
✓ Streamlined case management and strong workflow
✓ Available from anywhere with internet connection
✓ Point and click interface is extremely easy to learn and use

YOU CAN DO THIS: Case management improvement is both do-able and affordable — regardless of the size of your non-profit.

**HERE IS WHAT TO DO NOW TO GET STARTED:**

It really is that simple. We make this process as easy as possible because we know that any kind of change in an organization can be challenging and perhaps a little scary. We are now in our second decade of serving people just like you — those who fight the tough fight, every day at their

> ### 1. Complete the worksheets.
>
> Remember, these are a guide to help you, not a strict test that has to be filled out perfectly. For some, it is as simple as jotting down some notes and thoughts; others choose to print out the sheets and make it a staff activity. Either way, the important part is to take action toward your goal of better client care.

agencies, and we completely understand how seriously you take your mission to serve your clients. You don't want to do anything to jeopardize or degrade what you already deliver for your clients. Our gentle approach is intended to make sure "FAMCare" is the right solution for you and also that you are comfortable with every step of the process.

We wish you all success on your journey to improve case management for you clients and front-line caseworkers.

Oh, and by the way: DON'T FORGET TO CHECK OUT OUR PAGE "WHAT OUR CLIENTS SAY…" AS WELL AS THE WORKSHEETS. YOU WILL FIND BOTH ON THE PAGES THAT FOLLOW.

**2. Contact us.**

Our contact information is located in the Resource Section of this book.

Reach out to us when you are ready and we'll ask you some questions based on the worksheets (remember, this is not a test, we're just gathering information to make your assessment as productive as possible). Then, at your convenience, we can schedule the assessment.

**This is an Interactive Book with Free Videos, Case Studies and Other Useful Tools!**

Please register by visiting the website, register, introduce yourself, share what you do and your biggest problem that you'd like to tackle with information management.

On this site you can see free videos and an opportunity to get a free, one-hour consultation (a $150 value) with a seasoned, FAMCare specialist.

Visit: http://try.famcare.net/megaresources
or send an email to: info@globalvisiontech.com
or call: 678-965-6821

# CHAPTER EIGHT

## Bonus Material

### *Checklists and Worksheets: A full-size version of this assessment and others can be downloaded at:*
*www.famcare.net/resources/worksheets.aspx*

**Worksheet #1 Baseline — Where are you now?**

1. How much time does it take to get a client's intake paperwork finished? (Or, if you currently use a software system, how long does it take to input data for a new client?).

2. What are the challenges you face when bringing a client aboard? Is it common for things to be missed?

3. How is access to crucial client information handled currently? Is it secure and efficient?

4. Draw a flowchart of a typical client as they move through your process. If you are on a paper and file folder system, is the tracking sufficient to meet your needs? If you are on a software system, is tracking available and efficient? (Hint: Pay special attention to mapping your intake process as completely as possible. Write down each step.)

5. What reporting and data does your current method of tracking cases allow? Is it efficient and does it allow you to track trends?

6. What key areas need to be reported that you find difficult to track?

7. What accountability do you currently have in place? How are flags raised if key data or documents are missing for clients? Are you able to track case manager performance and address weakness?

8. How long does it take to train caseworkers to handle cases with confidence — using your current methods?

## Worksheet #2 Finding Your Solution — Where Do You Want to Go?

1. List the most crucial information and documents that need to be collected from clients. Make multiple lists if necessary to cover all client types.

**2.** What improvements would you make to forms to improve efficiency?

**3.** Name at least two ways you could improve tracking client progress. List as many as you can come up with, but at least two. (Hint: If you have multiple departments, ask how they could better work together with better tracking and workflow).

4. What are some key statistics that would help you analyze and improve outcomes for your clients?

5. Do you currently have a budget for case management tools or software?

**6.** Are you audited? What could be done to make that process more efficient? Also, do you work closely with community advocates, judges, or other third-party partners? Would it be helpful for them to have access to some of your files?

**7.** Name at least two ways access to case management data could improve collaboration and client outcomes. (List as many as you can come up with, but at least two).

8. What reporting data or tools would increase your grant
   and fundraising options?

GEORGE RITACCO

# ENDORSEMENTS

FAMCare has enabled us to organize, consolidate, communicate, and legitimize our information on a whole new level. We will surely have a difficult time remembering how we were able to function without it!
**~ Scott Althauser, Director of Programs at No Longer Bound**

"FAMCare is easy to use, easy to customize, easy to implement, easy to train on, and the customer service is phenomenal. We have been supported every step of the way with great ideas and timely advice on how to create a system that works for us with our unique business needs. I would highly recommend FAMCare to anyone looking for an easily customizable case management database."
**~ Louise Angermann, Outcomes and Evaluations Manager, Lilliput**

"What we are accomplishing is a feat that I know many of our sister Caribbean states have been trying to accomplish. We are definitely blazing trails here and it seems we could not have asked for a better partner in GVT and FAMCare!"
**~Judith Alpuche, CEO Ministry of Belize – MHDSTPA**

"A major part of child welfare reform requires providers and child welfare workers to manage to outcomes. FAMCare has provided a cutting edge management information system to Nebraska."
**~ Dave Newell, CEO Nebraska Families Collaborative (NFC)**

"FAMCare has allowed us to eliminate the need for paper intakes, speeding up the overall intake process. The system has facilitated improved communications between caseworkers in multiple locations — which is a great advantage for how we serve our clients."
**~ Jennifer Trotter, Program Director, Harvest Foods and Outreach Center**

"I'm a quality manager at a social services organization that provides a range of services. We've been involved with GVT for the last fifteen years — customizing the FAMCare® platform for our purposes and have found it to be a great experience. We've managed now to automate most of our

clinical forms and have been able to get quick reliable data in terms of outcomes, utilization, customer satisfaction and risk management. I highly recommend the product!
~ **Dave Juedemann, (ECH)**

"GVT has a very effective training and implementation process and the customer support team is extremely responsive to our 1,000+ user base."
~**Sam Haddad, IT Director for (JAIS), Wayne County, MI**

## Other Websites
http://www.globalvisiontech.com

http://www.YouTube.com/GVTmedia

http://www.facebook.com/GVTinc

http://www.twitter.com/GVTinc

# BIBLIOGRAPHY

Applebaum, R., & Kunkel, S. (1991, February 1). Long-Term Care for the Boomers: A Public  Policy Challenge for the Twenty-first Century. Retrieved January 3, 2015.

Banham, R. (n.d.). Facing the Future. Retrieved January 8, 2015.

Barr, P. (2014, January 14). The Boomer Challenge. Retrieved January 4, 2015.

Benz, C. (2012, August 9). 50 Must Know Statistics about Long-Term Care. Retrieved January 11, 2015.

Bowser, B. (2013, March 1). Why Long-Term Care for U.S. Seniors is Headed for 'Crisis'. Retrieved January 3, 2015.

Colby, S., & Ortman, J. (2012, May 1). The Baby Boom Cohort in the US: 2012-2060. Retrieved January 14, 2015.

Evashwick, ScD, C., Frates, PhD, J., & Fahey, PhD, D. (2008, January 1). Long Term Care: An Essential Element of Health Administration Education.

FATE: Foundation Aiding the Elderly. (2013, January 1). Retrieved January 19, 2015.

Fowler, W. (2012, August 8). Responding to the Challenges of Long-Term Care. Retrieved January 5, 2015.

Frank, R. (2012, January 1). Long-Term Care in the U.S. Retrieved January 3, 2015.

Friedland, R. (2005, January 1). Selected LTC Statistics. Retrieved January 15, 2015

Harris-Kojetin, Ph.D., L., Sengupta, Ph.D., M., Park-Lee, Ph.D., E., & Valverde, M.P.H., R. (2013, January 1). Long-Term Care Services in the United States: 2013 Overview. Retrieved January 7, 2015.

How The Baby Boomer Generation Is Changing The U.S. Healthcare System. (2013, June 5). Retrieved February 5, 2015.

Institute for the Future of Aging Services. (2007, January 1). The Long-

Term Care Workforce: Can the Crisis be Fixed? Retrieved January 4, 2015

Johnson, R., Toohey, D., & Wiener, J. (2007, April 1). Meeting the Long-Term Care Needs of the Baby Boomers: How Changing Families Will Affect Paid Helpers and Institutions. Retrieved January 6, 2015.

Kane, J. (2013, November 6). 6 Tips for Averting America's Looming LTC Crisis. Retrieved January 7, 2015.

Leopardo, M. (2013, May 1). How the ACA Affects Health Care Construction. Retrieved February 5, 2015.

Long-Term Care: Facilities Based Services. (2011, January 1). Retrieved January 5, 2015.

Long Term Care Insurance Statistics: October 2014 Update. (2014, October 1). Retrieved January 10, 2015.

Orestis, C. (2014, January 10). 2014: A Critical year for the Future of Long-Term Care in America. Retrieved January 7, 2015.

Reid, T. (2015, January 1). Where's the War on Alzheimer's? *AARP Bulletin*, pp. Pp 15-20.

Rill, L. (2012, January 1). New Areas of Reform on the Long-Term Care Labor Force Crisis. Retrieved January 16, 2015.

SCAN Foundation: The State of LTC Financing. (2013, January 1). Retrieved January 6, 2015.

SCAN Foundation: Where is it provided. (2012, October 1). Retrieved January 3, 2015.

SCAN Foundation: Who Pays for LTC in the U.S? (2013, January 16). Retrieved January 5, 2015.

SCAN Foundation: Who Provides LTC in the US? (2012, October 1). Retrieved January 3, 2015.

Selected Long-Term Care Statistics. (2005, January 1). Retrieved January 1, 2015.

SPAN, P. (2013, January 9). Even Fewer Geriatricians in Training. *New*

*York Times.*

Statistical Abstract of the U.S. 2012. (2012, January 1). Retrieved January 12, 2015.

2012 Physician Specialty Data Book Center for Workforce Studies. (2012, November 1). Retrieved January 10, 2015.

U.S. Long-Term Care Workforce at a Glance. (2010, January 1). Retrieved January 5, 2015

www.ingramcontent.com/pod-product-compliance
Lightning Source LLC
Chambersburg PA
CBHW060939050326
40690CB00011B/1507